B A L A N C E   Q U E S T

A Numeric Progression Puzzle

By:

W. Whit Mc Mahan

authorHOUSE®

AuthorHouse™
1663 Liberty Drive
Bloomington, IN 47403
www.authorhouse.com
Phone: 1-800-839-8640

Published by AuthorHouse   08/24/2012

ISBN: 978-1-4772-6409-6 (sc)
ISBN: 978-1-4772-6408-9 (e)

Library of Congress Control Number: 2012915710

Any people depicted in stock imagery provided by Thinkstock are models, and such images are being used for illustrative purposes only.
Certain stock imagery © Thinkstock.

This book is printed on acid-free paper.

Introduction

A **Balance Quest (BQ)** puzzle is a grid of rectangles (or "boxes") arranged in a hierarchical fashion. Some of the rectangles have positive or negative integers in them, while others are blank. The grid is divided into two shaded (grey) end regions and one central white region, which are each further subdivided into rectangles (*See examples in the instructions sections*).

The objective of a Balance Quest puzzle is to fill in each blank rectangle with an integer in a way that "balances" the puzzle mathematically according to the puzzle rules. Solving the puzzle correctly requires knowledge of positive and negative addition.

There are three alternative puzzle grid sizes to suit the player, determined by the number of rectangles in the shaded regions, either: 16, 32, or 64. Therefore, the three available puzzle grid sizes are:

"BQ Sixteen" (small-grid)
"BQ Thirty-two" (medium-grid)
"BQ Sixty-four" (large-grid)

Puzzle Rules:

The puzzler's job is to enter either a positive or negative integer into each "blank" rectangular box in such a way that:

1. The value in each white box equals the sum of its adjoining half-height boxes.
2. Based on puzzle size, the shaded boxes must <u>include all</u> non-zero integers from either:
   a. -8 to 8 (for small-grid puzzles)
   b. -16 to 16 (for medium-grid puzzles)
   c. -32 to 32 (for large-grid puzzles)
3. No duplicate numbers may exist among the white boxes, or among the shaded boxes, but duplicate numbers may exist between the white and shaded boxes.

A Balance Quest puzzle is a learning or mind-sharpening tool for ages 10+. In principle, as the mind quickly shifts between addition and searching for duplicate integers, the left (analytical) and right (intuitive) sections of the brain are exercised rapidly. A solution may begin in a simple way and become *tricky* as the puzzler progresses. Comparing the puzzler's solution to the actual solution may be quite surprising.

<u>**There is one correct solution to each puzzle.**</u> Solve time may range from five minutes up to hours for the large challenging puzzles. Please be sure to choose a pencil with a "good eraser".

Best of Luck...

Contents

Balance Quest

PART I - Puzzles

BQ Sixteen Instructions

Puzzle by: Whit McMahan

Date: 8/11/2012

Complete a **Balance Quest Sixteen** puzzle by filling in the empty boxes with positive and negative numbers in a way that balances the sums between all values in the grid.

Sample Puzzle:

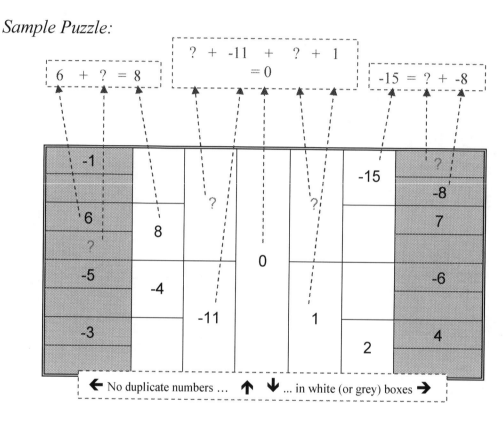

Puzzle Rules:

1. The value in each white box equals the sum of its adjoining half-height boxes (see examples within the dashed bubbles at top)

2. The shaded boxes include <u>all numbers</u> from -8 through 8, except 0.

3. No duplicate numbers may exist among the white boxes, or among the shaded boxes, but duplicate numbers may exist between the white and shaded boxes.

Please use a Pencil with an eraser.

Puzzle by: Whit McMahan

Date: 8/11/2012

Sample Puzzle Solution:

-1	7				-15	-7
8		15		-5		-8
6	8				10	7
2			0			3
-5	-4				-1	-6
1		-11		1		5
-3	-7				2	4
-4						-2

Get your Brain in Gear!

Easy Sixteen

PUZZLE#1

1	3				
		4			-4
-6			0	2	4
6				13	8
-5			5		
					-7

PUZZLE#2

1	-6				3
		-5		2	4
-4			0		7
2					
3					-3
	9				-5

PUZZLE#3

-3	-1				-2
				6	
-7			15		3
-5			0		4
	2				
		-8			1
-6					

Easy Sixteen

PUZZLE#4

-8					-5
2	-1		0		-1
-2		14		-2	-6
7	8		-6		-7

PUZZLE#5

8				-3	3
5	4		-18		-8
-2		0			1
6	1	-4			7

PUZZLE#6

8		2		-4	1
3	-5		-6		-7
4		0		6	-2
6					-2

Easy Sixteen

PUZZLE#7

2						
-12	-2				4
-5		0			-6
1	-1			15	-1
-8				9	3

PUZZLE#8

-8	-11				-4
-1	-18	0			1
7	15				3
5			-2	2	4

PUZZLE#9

1	7				-2
2	5		8	2	3
4		0			-3
-6	-14				7

Easy Sixteen

PUZZLE#10

7	10					-4
-6		-1				-3
-8			0		13	5
2	8			7		1

PUZZLE#11

-3					3	5
-7				-11		-6
-5			0		6	2
		-4				8
-1	-5					

PUZZLE#12

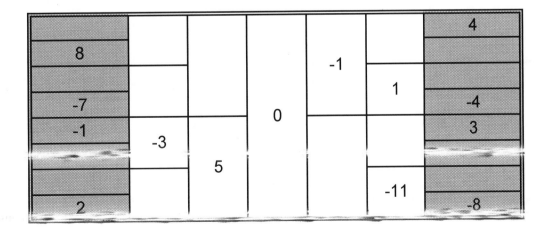

8				-1		4
-7			0		1	-4
-1	-3					3
		5			-11	
2						-8

Par Sixteen

PUZZLE#13

1	9			5		6
					1	
-8			0			-6
3						2
-5					2	
						5

PUZZLE#14

-2						
	7					-3
6						-6
5			0			-7
		6			-15	
3	5					4

PUZZLE#15

1					10	7
			-1			
-5			0			-7
4	1	5				6
-1						8

Par Sixteen

PUZZLE#16

						3
-8				13		
4			0		9	7
-5	-8					-6
-2		-14				6

PUZZLE#17

					9	4
-6				15		
7			0			8
-1	1					-5
		-2				
-4						-3

PUZZLE#18

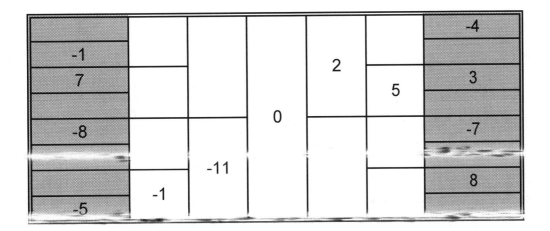

				2		-4
-1					5	3
7			0			
-8						-7
	-1	-11				8
-5						

Par Sixteen

PUZZLE#19

-2				-1	-6
4				-2	-5
1	-6	-17	0		5
					8
-8					

PUZZLE#20

3					5
-1					
-6	-8	-5	0	13	4
-5			12		7
					-3

PUZZLE#21

-4				3	-3
3			13		
1			0		8
		-18			4
-5	-13				-2

Par Sixteen

PUZZLE#22

1	-3				2	-5
5		8		-5		-6
-2			0			-3
4						8

PUZZLE#23

-8	-4					3
1		-9				-3
2			0			5
7				4	1	-7

PUZZLE#24

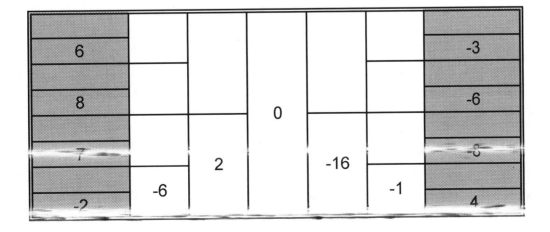

6						-3
8			0			-6
7	-6	2		-16	-1	-6
-2						4

Challenging Sixteen

PUZZLE#25

7	1	-3				6
-3	-6		0			-8
-7						-2
5						-5

PUZZLE#26

5					1	-5
-6			0	-5		1
-4						-2
8					5	2

PUZZLE#27

8						3
-5			0			6
2	-5	-8				7
-1					-1	5

Challenging Sixteen

PUZZLE#28

3						-5
4	-4		0			-1
8		11				2
6	2					7

PUZZLE#29

-1						4
5			0			2
-2		-5				7
-4	-9				-4	3

PUZZLE#30

-8		-4				-7
-3	5		0			-4
3						-2
-6					-3	-5

Challenging Sixteen

PUZZLE#31

-4	-9					-7
2			0			-1
1		12				
8	14					-8
						-6

PUZZLE#32

4						
2					-1	1
	5		0			6
7		-4				8
-6						-8

PUZZLE#33

5	-2					-1
7		2				
			0			-8
1					10	2
-2						
						-4

Challenging Sixteen

PUZZLE#34

5						1
4	-3		0			6
-6	-4	-11				3
-5						-3

PUZZLE#35

5						-7
1	-5		0		11	-3
-2				-1		8
-5						-4

PUZZLE#36

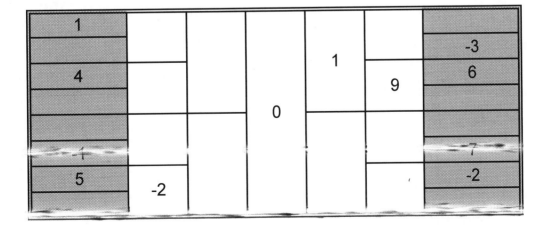

1				1		-3
4			0		9	6
-1						-7
5	-2					-2

BQ Thirty-two Instructions

Puzzle by: Whit McMahan

Date 8/11/2012

Complete a **Balance Quest Thirty-two** puzzle by filling in the empty boxes with positive and negative numbers in a way that balances the sums between all values in the grid.

Sample Puzzle:

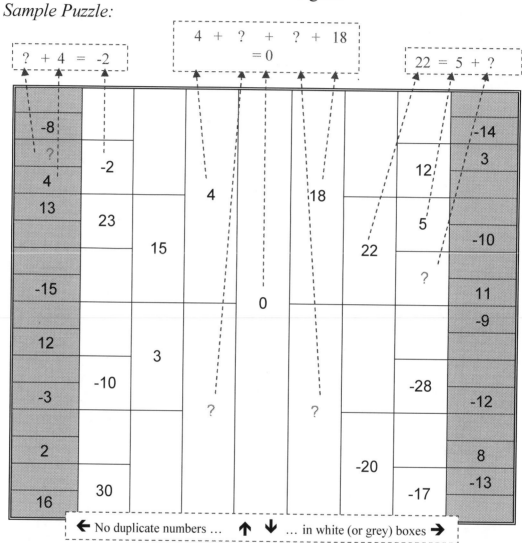

← No duplicate numbers … ↑ ↓ … in white (or grey) boxes →

Puzzle Rules:

1. The value in each white box equals the sum of its adjoining half-height boxes (see examples within the dashed bubbles at top)

2. The shaded boxes include <u>all numbers</u> from -16 through 16, except 0.

3. No duplicate numbers may exist among the white boxes, or among the shaded boxes, but duplicate numbers may exist between the white and shaded boxes.

Please use a pencil with an eraser.

BQ Thirty-two Instructions

Puzzle by: Whit McMahan   Date 8/11/2012

Sample Puzzle Solution:

-1	-9						-16	-2
-8		-11				-4		-14
-6	-2						12	3
4			4	18				9
13	23					5		15
10		15			22			-10
7	-8					17		6
-15			0					11
1	13					-14		-9
12		3			-42			-5
-7	-10					-28		-16
-3			40	-62				-12
5	7					-3		-11
2		37			-20			8
14	30					-17		-13
16								-4

Par Four

Easy Thirty-two

PUZZLE#37

```
 2    -4
      -15          -16
-12               -50   -24  -11
 8                            -5
13    10                      -2
 3    15                11     4
-9    22           0         2  10
-15        1    39          25  11
-14   -16                        7
```

PUZZLE#38

```
 1           8                -29  -16
11    18                -26
10         28                   5   5
 8    22           0           3
 9
-3    9           -25           -1
13   -12          -56   -16    -5
-7                      -23    -10
                               -14
                                -8
```

Easy Thirty-two

PUZZLE#39

12	-9		-3		-56	-21	2		-16
3		-2					-15		-3
10	-19			0					-14
-13									-9
13	4						12		-5
14	22					1	-6		1
6									-8
4									-2

PUZZLE#40

5	8	32					-5		7
9	2			0		-17			-2
6									-8
12						13	-2		2
-14	7		-66	60					11
-7	-18	-43					29		-3
-5									8
-10									16

Page 19

Easy Thirty-two

PUZZLE#41

8	3						-29	-16
			-28			-30		4
-4								5
-15		-40						2
-7	-15			0				
-11								3
6	15				13		-10	-9
-6	-20	8				22	24	-12
12								11

PUZZLE#42

-11	-15	-9					-2	7
								-12
4								
8								12
-7	-23			0			-11	-5
10						23		-3
-1	14		-10	66			10	1
-8		-32						14
-13	-27						24	11

Easy Thirty-two

PUZZLE#43

-4								
-5	-18	-33					3	15
4			-31	69				1
-6	10				37	13		13
-2				0				5
-9	-16				14	-4		12
-15						-3		-14
-16	-13							7
								9

PUZZLE#44

-7								-10
-8					5	23		8
13	14	3			8	15		7
-5				0				-1
-9	-5	-14				16		10
2			-20					-3
-12					9	-1		-4
-5	19							-2

Easy Thirty-two

PUZZLE#45

-14							-2	3
13	2					-25		-7
2	6			-33				-8
9							-7	-6
12	13		0					5
-15		4				-12		-10
-13	-3	27			3			-9
11						24		8

PUZZLE#46

-10						-18	-6
12	27			-55			3
13	14				-16		-14
11					-25		4
-11	-2	28	0		15		7
16		-6				5
-8	-24			13		10
-3				8		6

Easy Thirty-two

PUZZLE#47

									15
-1	-5						27		
7								11	3
14	7								12
								-8	-6
2			0					-13	-3
-11									
11	-4								9
			-33		-16			20	4
6		-31				-7			
-12	-21								-13

PUZZLE#48

									5
-11	-20					9			
6				30			-7		-8
12		40							-14
10	13				0			-25	-12
13							23		14
									-1
2	-4				21				
-4	-9					6	24		16
									-3
7									

Par Thirty-two

PUZZLE#49

								27	
						28			11
-5									
-8					16				14
9	-1								-15
6							7		13
-7	-2			0					7
3		2				9		-10	4
			-6					-28	-16
-3									
-11	-13								10

PUZZLE#50

-15	-5								-6
-5								2	15
-7									7
-9	-10							-8	6
3	5			0					16
		19						-4	-12
9			20		34				
-3							-14	-4
-11	3					9			12

Par Thirty-two

PUZZLE#51

9	1	24					-22	-6
11								1
6							-24	-14
3				0				-9
-3	11					9		10
-7					-2			-15
15			-6		19		18	13
		2						
-11	-15							8

PUZZLE#52

-5	-4						-7	-16
16			42	-8				6
3		17				-1		-3
12	27				-15			-6
14	13		0			-3		-10
-14								-2
								-12
-15								
10	21					-6		11

Par Thirty-two

PUZZLE#53

11								
		25				-41		-16
-3	-2				-23		-16	
			32					-12
12							12	9
-2	3							
				0				13
-11							-3	
6						16		-10
	20							4
-6	-21							
								10
2								8

PUZZLE#54

-13	-20							
3		-27				-29		-11
			-25				-14	-6
-1								
6	8							-9
							-4	
13				0				11
							14	10
-16								5
					44			15
-2							29	
						24		
-12	4							-14

Page 26

Par Thirty-two

4							21	13
-8	-3					26		14
-6				0				16
-7	-19							11
-2	-18		-25		-31			6
-3							3	-4
10		7				-30		3
-14	-5						-28	-15

16	15							-10
-12			8		-11		13	4
11	21	3				1	9	-4
-7				0				-5
7	-9						4	6
-9								12
14							-27	-14
3	-3							5

Par Thirty-two

PUZZLE#57

-9		-30				-5		-10
3	-10		-6	-14			-1	11
16	10						3	-1
13				0				-14
9	16	5						8
5							4	-8
-15	-22							14
-3								-2

PUZZLE#58

2						3		10
-12	-14			14		6		-8
3						19		4
-3	-12			0				-15
11		-15				17		8
-14	-19		13					6
13								-10
5	21					-4		12

Par Thirty-two

PUZZLE#59

13	-6			-32		-27	-29	10
6								-16
-2								
-9	-15			0			-10	8
15	24							-11
14			49				-14	2
16		16					-3	-4
-7	-4							11
								7

PUZZLE#60

-1	-16			-32		-17	16
1							-14
12	6				-26		-4
5			0		-11		-13
15	23						-12
10		25			20		6
-16	-18	-1			18		7
							3

Page 29

Challenging Thirty-two

PUZZLE#61

							-1
-15					33		
-13	2					30	14
7							-10
-4				0			-8
-2							-11
-3	10				-25	-5	9
		12		-11			-5
-12	-19	-4				1	
12							11

PUZZLE#62

							-14
14		22					
13	21						-9
-7	2						-8
-6							
				0			-1
15					27	16	5
-2	-17			32			16
-11	-4	-24					2
		-32				7	
-16							4

Page 30

Challenging Thirty-two

PUZZLE#63

								2
-1						15	9	
-15	-25							-8
-9								9
1			0					3
6		8						-13
15	13		46	-38		-9		-3
4								-12
8	24				-28	-12		-5

PUZZLE#64

-2	-1							2
-10								8
6		5						4
-1	15			0				-9
3		29						-11
5	12		57	-52		-4		-15
	22							-3
9					-30			-14
-4						-19		

Challenging Thirty-two

PUZZLE#65

12   8   -14   -25   4
-10   7
-11   -1
-3   -2
-13   0
-3   -6
-9   6   -44
6   -24
-32   -16
6   19   -5
42
24   8
9

PUZZLE#66

2
-7   -3
7   -12   -1
-22   -12
-6
9   -13
0
14   18   15
32   16
-14   -17
20   23
3   12
-10   15
11   -13
-9

Challenging Thirty-two

PUZZLE#67

5								-3
11						-23		-14
6						-9		2
14	27			0				-13
-8						36		15
-2	-1		-20		9	5		-7
-5						-8		-16
-12	-18	-14						-15

PUZZLE#68

13		29				-22		-9
16	27		47		-33	-23		-8
-4						-3		7
-5	7			0				-13
1		-6						-2
-12	-9							6
-6						-17		-14
9								1

Challenging Thirty-two

PUZZLE#69

9 | 25 | 21 | 37 | 0 | -19 | -20 | -5 | 4
-11 | | | | | | | -13 | -15
-4 | 14 | | | | | | -2 | -10
-1 | | | | | | | | -5
-8 | | | | | | | | -16
1 | | | | | | | | -7
11 | | | | | | | | -6
-9 | -22 | | | | | | 8 | 5

PUZZLE#70

-11 | -1 | -8 | 7 | 0 | -26 | 16 | 21 | 9
-2 | 10 | | | | | | -25 | 10
7 | | | | | | | | -13
-9 | | | | | | | | -1
| | | | | | | | 8
-5 | | | | | | | 9 | -6
-7 | | | | | | | -12 | -14
5 | | | | | | 17 | | 13
6 | | | | | | | |

Challenging Thirty-two

PUZZLE#71

-6
-5
-6
-29
13
-14
-1
29
28
-8
15
5
-4
0
1
12
-2
-12
-1
-10
24
14
-2
20
-15
18
2

PUZZLE#72

7
16
-6
8
-7
-12
-5
6
4
13
11
0
3
-12
19
-8
23
8
-3
-24
-9
-4
-17
5
-18
-25
-1
-9

Balance Quest Sixty-four Instructions

Puzzle by: Whit McMahan

Date: 8/11/2012

Complete a **Balance Quest Sixty-four** puzzle by filling in the empty boxes with positive and negative numbers in a way that balances the sums between all values in the grid.

Sample Puzzle:

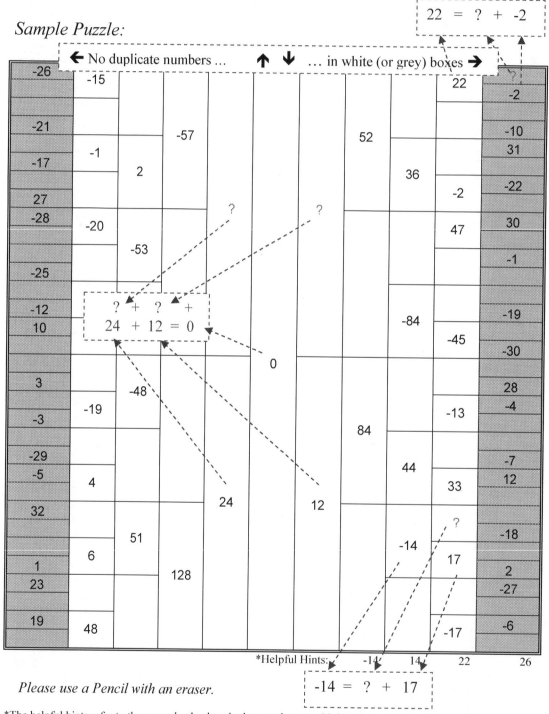

← No duplicate numbers ... ↑ ↓ ... in white (or grey) boxes →

$$22 = ? + -2$$

$$? + ? +$$
$$24 + 12 = 0$$

Please use a Pencil with an eraser.

Helpful Hints: -14 14 22 26

$$-14 = ? + 17$$

*The helpful hints refer to the unresolved values in the grey boxes, which you may find useful as you progress.

Balance Quest Sixty-four Instructions

Puzzle by: Whit McMahan

Date: 8/11/2012

Puzzle Rules:

1. The value in each white box equals the sum of its adjoining half-height boxes (see examples within the dashed bubbles)

2. The shaded boxes include <u>all numbers</u> from -32 through 32, except 0.

3. No duplicate numbers may exist among the white boxes, or among the shaded boxes, but duplicate numbers may exist between the white and shaded boxes.

Sample Puzzle Solution:

-26	-15							22	24
11		-59					16		-2
-23	-44						-6		4
-21			-57			52			-10
16	-1							38	31
-17		2					36		7
-24	3			-64	28			-2	-22
27									20
-28	-20							47	30
8		-53					60		17
-8	-33							13	-1
-25			-7			-24			14
26	14							-39	-20
-12		46					-84		-19
10	32							-45	-15
22				0					-30
-32	-29							53	25
3		-48					40		28
-16	-19							-13	-4
-3			-104			84			-9
-31	-60							11	18
-29		-56					44		-7
-5	4							33	12
9				24	12				21
32	45							-31	-13
13		51					-14		-18
5	6							17	15
1			128			-72			2
23	29							-41	-27
6		77					-58		-14
19	48							-17	-6
29									-11

Page 37

Easy Sixty-four

PUZZLE #73

-26	-15		-57					52		22	-2
-21											-10
-17	-1	2							36		31
27										-2	-22
-28	-20	-53								47	30
-25											-1
-12									-84		-19
10				0						-45	-30
3	-19	-48						84		-13	28
-3									44		-4
-29	4									33	-7
-5			24		12						12
32	6	51							-14	17	-18
1		128									2
23											-27
19	48									-17	-6

Helpful Hints: 14   22   26

Easy Sixty-four

-5	24							43	31
3		47							14
22					107				23
-4	11					26	-29		-13
-23			4				6		9
11	13					-5			7
-24		-94					42		16
-11	-41	-57							-12
-20			0				28		30
-15	-22	-52				14			-8
-1	12								4
10							-44		-25
-9	8			-63			27		6
-32		-53				-18			-14
19	20				-64				-22
-26							-49		-28

Helpful Hints: -17   5   28

Par Sixty-four

-28									50	27
32	39							87		28
30	52	53								16
-9									-2	19
-3	-14		97					-1	-25	
20		27					-4		1	
-13		51			-37			-40	-26	
-12	6								5	
-29			0						-7	
-27	-58	-103					-8	-22		
6					-22	2	-2			
-20						-36	-8			
26	16		-89							
25	54				-23	-17	15			
8							11			
12	-12					-20	-15			
							-1			

Helpful Hints: -19   -6   3   17

Par Sixty-four

PUZZLE #76

-10	18								-24
-29						20			11
-26	-10	21			49		15		-15
26							6		32
-16				12			-6		-25
-27					-3				10
8	-5	4					-21		-8
9									-20
31			0			8			-4
20	42				-32				-23
-12	-18	-68				17			14
-18			117						-22
-11	19	32				-8			23
15		95		-55					-28
24					-17				2
27	26			-16					-5

Helpful Hints: -30   -21   18   25

Page 41

Ultimate Challenge

7									37	23
	-15	-33								
-26						106				30
-7								42		22
-29	-53						50			
										13
-2								-49		-27
-1										-20
-19	-50									-23
9							-4			
				0				7		28
29		91								32
31	57		101			35	40	25		24
-4	-1							4		-14
21			45		89					4
15		-12					6	14		-3
-12	-21									8
2	-30									19
									2	
-30										-8

Helpful Hints: -28   -18   -15   6   25

Balance Quest

PART II – Puzzle Solutions

BQ Sixteen Puzzle Solutions

Easy Sixteen Solutions

PUZZLE#1
SOLUTION

1	3			-7	-3
2		4	-5		-4
7	1			2	-2
-6			0		4
3	9			13	5
6		-4	5		8
-5	-13			-8	-1
-8					-7

PUZZLE#2
SOLUTION

-7	-6			3	-1
1		-5	2		4
5	1			-1	7
-4			0		-8
2	10			-9	-6
8		19	-16		-3
3	9			-7	-2
6					-5

PUZZLE#3
SOLUTION

2	-1			6	-2
-3		-3	15		8
5	-2			9	6
-7			0		3
-5	2			3	4
7		-8	-4		-1
-4	-10			-7	1
-6					-8

Easy Sixteen Solutions

PUZZLE#4
SOLUTION

-4	-12	-13			1	6
-8			5			-5
-3	-1			4		5
2		0			-1
8	6	14		-2	4
-2			-6		-6
7	8			-4	3
1					-7

PUZZLE#5
SOLUTION

8	10	14		-18	-3	-6
2					3
5	4			-15	-7
-1		0			-8
-2	-5			5	1
-3		-4	8		4
6	1			3	7
-5					-4

PUZZLE#6
SOLUTION

8	7	2		-6	-4	-5
-1					1
-8	-5			-2	5
3		0			-7
-6	-10			6	4
-4		-7	11		2
6	3			5	-2
-3					7

Easy Sixteen Solutions

PUZZLE#7
SOLUTION

2	10	-2	0	-9	1	-3
8	10	-2	0	-9	1	4
-7	-12	-2	0	-9	-10	-6
-5	-12	-2	0	-9	-10	-4
-2	-1	-4	0	15	6	7
1	-1	-4	0	15	6	-1
5	-3	-4	0	15	9	3
-8	-3	-4	0	15	9	6

PUZZLE#8
SOLUTION

-3	-11	-18	0	-6	-9	-5
-8	-11	-18	0	-6	-9	-4
-6	-7	-18	0	-6	3	2
-1	-7	-18	0	-6	3	1
7	15	26	0	-2	-4	3
8	15	26	0	-2	-4	-7
6	11	26	0	-2	2	-2
5	11	26	0	-2	2	4

PUZZLE#9
SOLUTION

6	7	5	0	8	6	-2
1	7	5	0	8	6	8
2	-2	5	0	8	2	3
-4	-2	5	0	8	2	-1
4	-3	-17	0	4	-8	-3
-7	-3	-17	0	4	-8	-5
-8	-14	-17	0	4	12	5
-6	-14	-17	0	4	12	7

PUZZLE#10
SOLUTION

3	10	-1	0	-4	-5	-4
7	10	-1	0	-4	-5	-1
-5	-11	-1	0	-4	1	4
-6	-11	-1	0	-4	1	-3
-2	-10	-2	0	7	13	8
-8	-10	-2	0	7	13	5
2	8	-2	0	7	-6	-7
6	8	-2	0	7	-6	1

PUZZLE#11
SOLUTION

7	4	-2	0	-11	3	5
-3	4	-2	0	-11	3	-2
-7	-6	-2	0	-11	-14	-6
1	-6	-2	0	-11	-14	-8
-5	1	-4	0	17	6	4
6	1	-4	0	17	6	2
-4	-5	-4	0	17	11	8
-1	-5	-4	0	17	11	3

PUZZLE#12
SOLUTION

7	15	3	0	-1	-2	4
8	15	3	0	-1	-2	-6
-5	-12	3	0	-1	1	5
-7	-12	3	0	-1	1	-4
-1	-3	5	0	-7	4	3
-2	-3	5	0	-7	4	1
6	8	5	0	-7	-11	-3
2	8	5	0	-7	-11	-8

Par Sixteen Solutions

PUZZLE#13
SOLUTION

Col 1	Col 2	Col 3	Col 4	Col 5	Col 6	Col 7
1	9				4	6
8		-3		5		-2
-4	-12		0		1	7
-8						-6
3	-4				6	2
-7		-10		8		4
-5	-6				2	-3
-1						5

PUZZLE#14
SOLUTION

Col 1	Col 2	Col 3	Col 4	Col 5	Col 6	Col 7
-2	-3				-8	-5
-1		4		-6		-3
1	7		0		2	-6
6						8
5	1				-15	-7
-4		6		-4		-8
2	5				11	4
3						7

PUZZLE#15
SOLUTION

Col 1	Col 2	Col 3	Col 4	Col 5	Col 6	Col 7
1	-5				10	7
-6		-18		-1		3
-8	-13		0		-11	-4
-5						-7
-3	1				8	2
4		5		14		6
5	4				6	-2
-1						8

Par Sixteen Solutions

PUZZLE#16
SOLUTION

-1	-9	3	0	13	4	3
-8	-9	3	0	13	4	1
4	12	3	0	13	9	7
8	12	3	0	13	9	2
-5	-8	-14	0	-2	-13	-6
-3	-8	-14	0	-2	-13	-7
-2	-6	-14	0	-2	11	6
-4	-6	-14	0	-2	11	5

PUZZLE#17
SOLUTION

-8	-14	-4	0	15	9	4
-6	-14	-4	0	15	9	5
3	10	-4	0	15	6	-2
7	10	-4	0	15	6	8
-1	1	-2	0	-9	-12	-5
2	1	-2	0	-9	-12	-7
1	-3	-2	0	-9	3	6
-4	-3	-2	0	-9	3	-3

PUZZLE#18
SOLUTION

-3	-4	8	0	2	-3	-4
-1	-4	8	0	2	-3	1
7	12	8	0	2	5	3
5	12	8	0	2	5	2
-8	-10	-11	0	1	-13	-7
-2	-10	-11	0	1	-13	-6
4	-1	-11	0	1	14	8
-5	-1	-11	0	1	14	6

PUZZLE#19
SOLUTION

-2	-3	3		-1	1	7
-1	-3	3		-1	1	-6
4	6	3		-1	-2	3
2	6	3	0	-1	-2	-5
1	-6	-17	0	15	11	6
-7	-6	-17	0	15	11	5
-3	-11	-17		15	4	8
-8	-11	-17		15	4	-4

PUZZLE#20
SOLUTION

-7	-4	-13		6	1	5
3	-4	-13		6	1	-4
-1	-9	-13		6	5	1
-8	-9	-13	0	6	5	4
-6	-8	-5	0	12	13	7
-2	-8	-5	0	12	13	6
-5	3	-5		12	-1	-3
8	3	-5		12	-1	2

PUZZLE#21
SOLUTION

-4	-11	-9		13	3	-3
-7	-11	-9		13	3	6
3	2	-9		13	10	2
-1	2	-9	0	13	10	8
1	-5	-18	0	14	9	4
-6	-5	-18	0	14	9	5
-8	-13	-18		14	5	7
-5	-13	-18		14	5	-2

Par Sixteen Solutions

PUZZLE#22
SOLUTION

1	-3				2	7
-4		8		-5		-5
6	11				-7	-1
5			0			-6
-2	-9				-11	-3
-7		-2		-1		-8
3	7				10	8
4						2

PUZZLE#23
SOLUTION

4	-4				2	3
-8		-9		-6		-1
-6	-5				-8	-3
1			0			-5
2	-2				3	5
-4		11		4		-2
6	13				1	8
7						-7

PUZZLE#24
SOLUTION

5	11				-4	-1
6		21		-7		-3
2	10				-3	3
8			0			-6
1	8				-15	-7
-7		2		-16		-8
-4	-6				-1	-5
-2						4

Challenging Sixteen Solutions

PUZZLE#25
SOLUTION

7	1	-3	0	3	8	6
-6	1				8	2
-1	-4				-5	3
-3	-4			3	-5	-8
1	-6	7			2	-2
-7	-6	7		-7	2	4
8	13				-9	-4
5	13				-9	-5

PUZZLE#26
SOLUTION

-1	4	-10	0	-5	1	6
5	4				1	-5
-6	-14				-6	1
-8	-14			-5	-6	-7
-3	-7	8			2	4
-4	-7	8		7	2	-2
8	15				5	3
7	15				5	2

PUZZLE#27
SOLUTION

8	5	-4	0	2	4	1
-3	5				4	3
-4	-9				-2	6
-5	-9			2	-2	-8
-7	-5	-8			11	7
2	-5	-8		10	11	4
-2	-3				-1	5
-1	-3				-1	-6

Challenging Sixteen Solutions

PUZZLE#28
SOLUTION

-2	1				-8	-3
3		-3		-15		-5
-8	-4				-7	-6
4			0			-1
1	9				-5	2
8		11		7		-7
-4	2				12	7
6						5

PUZZLE#29
SOLUTION

-1	7				5	4
8		9		-1		1
5	2				-6	-8
-3			0			2
-2	4				1	-6
6		-5		-3		7
-5	-9				-4	3
-4						-7

PUZZLE#30
SOLUTION

-8	-9				-2	-7
-1		-4		1		5
-3	5				3	7
8			0			-4
6	9				2	-2
3		4		-1		4
1	-5				-3	2
-6						-5

Challenging Sixteen Solutions

PUZZLE#31
SOLUTION

-5	-9	-4	0	3	-3	-7
-4	-9	-4	0	3	-3	4
3	5	-4	0	3	6	-1
2	5	-4	0	3	6	7
1	-2	12	0	-11	-10	-2
-3	-2	12	0	-11	-10	-8
8	14	12	0	-11	-1	-6
6	14	12	0	-11	-1	5

PUZZLE#32
SOLUTION

4	9	6	0	3	4	3
5	9	6	0	3	4	1
2	-3	6	0	3	-1	-7
-5	-3	6	0	3	-1	6
-2	5	-4	0	-5	7	8
7	5	-4	0	-5	7	-1
-3	-9	-4	0	-5	-12	-8
-6	-9	-4	0	-5	-12	-4

PUZZLE#33
SOLUTION

-7	-2	2	0	1	5	-1
5	-2	2	0	1	5	6
7	4	2	0	1	-4	4
-3	4	2	0	1	-4	-8
-6	-5	-12	0	9	10	2
1	-5	-12	0	9	10	8
-2	-7	-12	0	9	-1	3
-5	-7	-12	0	9	-1	-4

Challenging Sixteen Solutions

PUZZLE#34
SOLUTION

5	1				9	8
-4		-2		14		1
-7	-3				5	-1
4			0			6
2	-4				-5	-8
-6		-11		-1		3
-5	-7				4	7
-2						-3

PUZZLE#35
SOLUTION

5	7				-3	-7
2		2		-7		4
1	-5				-4	-1
-6			0			-3
7	5				11	3
-2		6		-1		8
6	1				-12	-8
-5						-4

PUZZLE#36
SOLUTION

1	-3				-8	-5
-4		3		1		-3
4	6				9	6
2			0			3
-6	-7				15	8
		-9		5		7
5	-2				-10	-2
-7						-8

BQ Thirty-two Puzzle Solutions

Easy Thirty-two Solutions

PUZZLE#37
SOLUTION

-6	-4	-15	18	0	-58	-50	-26	-16
2								-10
1	-11						-24	-11
-12								-13
15	23	33				-8	-12	-7
8								-5
-3	10						4	6
13								-2
12	15	22	1		39	11	9	5
3								4
-9	7						2	10
16								-8
-15	-16	-21				28	25	11
-1								14
-14	-5						3	7
9								-4

PUZZLE#38
SOLUTION

1	-10	8	28	0	-7	-26	-29	-16
-11								-13
7	18						3	-2
11								5
10	-2	20				19	5	3
-12								2
14	22						14	15
8								-1
9	21	9	35		-56	-25	-9	-4
12								-5
-3	-12						-16	-10
-9								-6
16	29	26				-31	-8	-14
13								6
4	-3						-23	-8
-7								-15

Easy Thirty-two Solutions

PUZZLE#39
SOLUTION

12	8						-23	-16
-4		-1				-21		-7
3	-9						2	-3
-12			-3	-56				5
10	17					-15		-14
7		-2				-35		-1
-13	-19						-20	-9
-6				0				-11
13	28						3	8
15		32				15		-5
-10	4						12	1
14			43	16				11
6	22						-6	2
16		11				1		-8
4	-11						7	9
-15								-2

PUZZLE#40
SOLUTION

5	8						-5	-12
3		32				-8		7
9	24						-3	-1
15			35	-29				-2
6	2					-17		-8
-4		3				-21		-9
12	1						-4	-6
-11				0				2
-16	-30						15	4
-14		-23				13		11
14	7						-2	-3
-7			-66	60				1
-5	-18						18	10
-13		-43				47		8
-15	-25						29	13
-10								16

PUZZLE#41
SOLUTION

8	9						-29	-16
1		12				-30		-13
7	3		-28		-12		-1	-5
-4								4
-10	-25					18	2	5
-15		-40						-3
-8	-15						16	2
-7			0					14
-11	4						1	-2
15		19				-9		3
9	15		27		13		-10	-1
6								-9
-6	-20						-2	10
-14		8				22		-12
16	28						24	11
12								13

PUZZLE#42
SOLUTION

-11	-15						-2	7
-4		-9				-24		-9
2	6		-39		-17		-22	-12
4								-10
8	-7					18	6	6
-15		-30				7		12
-7	-23						-11	-6
-16			0					-5
10	8						13	-3
-2		22				23		16
-1	14		-10		66		10	1
15								9
3	-5						19	14
-8		-32				43		5
-13	-27						24	11
-14								13

Easy Thirty-two Solutions

PUZZLE#43
SOLUTION

-4	-15						29	14
-11		-33			32			15
-5	-18		-31				3	2
-13				69		24		1
4	-8				37			11
-12		2					13	13
16	10		0					8
-6						18		5
-2	-5				14			6
-3		-21					-4	12
-9	-16		-57	19				10
-7						-3		-14
-15	-23				5			7
-8		-36					8	-10
-16	-13							9
3								-1

PUZZLE#44
SOLUTION

-7	4					-26		-10
11		-19			-3			-16
-8	-23		-16			23		8
-15				5				15
1	14				-7			-14
13		3						7
-6	-11			8		15		16
-5			0					-1
-9	-5				16			6
4		-14						10
-11	-9			22				9
2			-20		6			-3
-12	-25			31		-1		-4
-13		-6						3
14	19			9		10		-2
5								12

Page 63

Easy Thirty-two Solutions

PUZZLE#45
SOLUTION

-14	-17	-15	-4	0	-33	-25	-2	3
-3								-5
13	2						-23	-7
-11								-16
2	6	11				-8	-1	-8
4								7
-4	5						-7	-1
9								-6
12	13	4	27		10	7	19	5
1								14
6	-9						-12	-2
-15								-10
10	-3	23				3	-21	-12
-13								-9
11	26						24	8
15								16

PUZZLE#46
SOLUTION

-10	-11	16	37	0	-55	-30	-18	-12
-1								-6
12	27						-12	3
15								-15
1	14	21				-25	-16	-14
13								-2
11	7						-9	4
-4								-13
-11	-2	28	-6		24	11	15	7
9								8
14	30						-4	-9
16								5
-16	-24	-34				13	5	10
-8								-5
-3	-10						8	2
-7								6

Page 64

Easy Thirty-two Solutions

PUZZLE#47
SOLUTION

-4							16	15
-1	-5					27		1
7		-6					11	3
-8	-1		13		36			8
14	7						17	5
-7		19				9		12
10	12						-8	-6
2			0					-2
13	2						-13	-3
-11		-2				-9		-10
11	-4						4	-5
-15			-33		-16			9
-16	-10						20	4
6		-31				-7		16
-12	-21						-27	-14
-9								-13

PUZZLE#48
SOLUTION

-9							16	5
-11	-20					9		11
6		-10					-7	-8
4	10		30		-46			1
15	27						-30	-16
12		40				-55		-14
10	13						-25	-12
3			0					-13
13	11						23	14
-2		7				15		9
-6	-4						-8	-1
2			-5		21			-7
-4	-9						24	16
-5		-12				6		8
-10	-3						-18	-3
7								-15

Page 65

PUZZLE#49
SOLUTION

-5	-14						27	16
-9		-23			28			11
-1	-9						1	-13
-8			-3	16				14
-10	-1					-19		-15
9		20			-12			-4
15	21					7		-6
6			0					13
-7	-2						19	7
5		2			9			12
3	4					-10		-14
1			-6	-7				4
8	5					-28		-16
-3		-8			-16			-12
-11	-13					12		2
-2								10

PUZZLE#50
SOLUTION

-15	-5						-22	-6
10		-12			-20			-16
-2	-7					2		15
-5			-25	-29				-13
4	-3					-1		-8
-7		-13			-9			7
-9	-10					-8		-14
-1			0					6
3	5					29		16
2		19			25			13
5	14					-4		-12
9			20	34				8
-3	-2					-14		-4
1		1			9			-10
-11	3					23		12
14								11

PUZZLE#51
SOLUTION

9	1						-22	-6
-8		24				-34		-16
11	23						-12	-13
12			38		-51			1
6	4						-24	-10
-2		14				-17		-14
3	10						7	16
7				0				-9
-3	11						9	-1
14		-8				-2		10
-7	-19						-11	-15
-12			-6		19			4
15	17						18	5
2		2				21		13
-4	-15						3	-5
-11								8

PUZZLE#52
SOLUTION

-5	-4						-7	9
1		25				7		-16
16	29						14	8
13			42		-8			6
3	-10						-1	-3
-13		17				-15		2
15	27						-14	-8
12				0				-6
14	13						-3	-10
-1		-5				-12		7
-14	-18						-9	-7
-4			5		-39			-2
4	-11						-21	-12
-15		10				-27		-9
11	21						-6	5
10								-11

PUZZLE#53
SOLUTION

11	27					-41	-25	-9
16		25						-16
-3	-2						-16	-4
1			32		-23			-12
-8	4					18	12	3
12		7						9
-2	3			0			6	-7
5								13
-1	-12					16	-3	7
-11		8						-10
6	20						19	15
14			-24		15			4
-15	-21						5	-5
-6		-32				-1		10
-13	-11						-6	8
2								-14

PUZZLE#54
SOLUTION

-13	-20					-29	-15	-4
-7		-27						-11
3	-7						-14	-6
-10			-25		-45			-8
-1	-6					-16	-12	-9
-5		2						-3
6	8			0			-4	-15
2								11
12	25					20	14	4
13		17						10
8	-8						6	5
-16			26		44			1
7	5					24	29	15
-2		9						14
16	4						-5	9
-12								-14

PUZZLE#55
SOLUTION

4	19						21	8
15		16			26			13
5	-3		-10			5		-9
-8				66				14
-1	-7				17			1
-6		-26			40			16
-7	-19					23		12
-12			0					11
-16	-18					-4		6
-2		-32			-1			-10
-3	-14					3		7
-11			-25	-31				-4
10	12					-2		3
2		7			-30			-5
9	-5					-28		-13
-14								-15

PUZZLE#56
SOLUTION

-1	15						-25	-10
16		5			-12			-15
-12	-10		8			13		9
2				-11				4
10	21				9			13
11		3			1			-4
-11	-18					-8		-5
-7			0					-3
-16	-9					4		6
7		-26			31			-2
-9	-17					27		12
-8			-7	10				15
14	22					-27		-13
8		19			-21			-14
3	-3					6		1
-6								5

PUZZLE#57
SOLUTION

-11	-20	-30			-5	-4	6
-9							-10
3	-10		-6	-14		-1	-12
-13							11
-6	10	24			-9	3	-1
16							4
13	14		0			-12	2
1							-14
7	16	5			27	23	8
9							15
5	-11		-24	44		4	12
-16							-8
-7	-22	-29			17	9	-5
-15							14
-4	-7					8	10
-3							-2

PUZZLE#58
SOLUTION

-4	-2	-16			3	-3	-13
2							10
-2	-14		-26	14		6	14
-12							-8
-1	2	-10			11	19	4
3							15
-9	-12		0			-8	7
-3							-15
11	4	-15			12	17	8
-7							9
-14	-19		13	-1		-5	6
-5							-11
-6	7	28			-13	-9	-10
13							1
16	21					-4	-16
5							12

Par Thirty-two Solutions

PUZZLE#59
SOLUTION

12	25						2	-8
13		19				-27		10
6	-6						-29	-16
-12			7		-32			-13
-2	3						5	-3
5		-12				-5		8
-6	-15						-10	1
-9			0					-11
15	24						1	2
9		33				-13		-1
-5	9						-14	-10
14			49		-24			-4
4	20						-3	-14
16		16				-11		11
3	-4						-8	-15
-7								7

PUZZLE#60
SOLUTION

-15	-16						11	16
-1		-23				-6		-5
1	-7						-17	-14
-8			-21		-32			-3
12	6						-15	-4
-6		2				-26		-11
5	-4						-11	2
-9			0					-13
15	23						-22	-10
8		26				-2		-12
10	3						20	6
-7			25		28			14
-16	-16						18	11
-2		-1				30		7
13	17						12	3
4								9

Page 71

PUZZLE #61
SOLUTION

-16	-31						3	-1
-15		-29				33		4
-13	2						30	14
15			-22	21				16
7	17						-9	-10
10		7			-12			1
-6	-10						-3	5
-4				0				-8
-2	6						-20	-9
8		16			-25			-11
-3	10						-5	9
13			12	-11				-14
-7	-19						1	-5
-12		-4			14			6
3	15						13	11
12								2

PUZZLE #62
SOLUTION

-13	1						-8	-14
14		22				-20		6
13	21						-12	-9
8			19	-27				-3
-7	2						4	-8
9		-3			-7			12
-6	-5						-11	-10
1				0				-1
10	25						16	11
15		8			27			5
-2	-17						11	-5
-15			-24	32				16
7	-4						-2	-4
-11		-32			5			2
-12	-28						7	3
-16								4

PUZZLE#63
SOLUTION

Col1	Col2	Col3	Col4	Col5	Col6	Col7	Col8	Col9
5	4						9	2
-1		-21				15		7
-15	-25		-34		26		6	-8
-10								14
11	2						22	13
-9		-13				11		9
-16	-15						-11	3
1			0					-14
6	-5						-1	12
-11		8				-10		-13
15	13				-38		-9	-6
-2			46					-3
4	14						-16	-12
10		38				-28		-4
8	24						-12	-5
16								-7

PUZZLE#64
SOLUTION

Col1	Col2	Col3	Col4	Col5	Col6	Col7	Col8	Col9
-2	-1						14	2
1		-17				9		12
-6	-16		-12		7		-5	8
-10								-13
-16	-10						19	4
6		5				-2		15
-1	15						-21	-9
16			0					-12
3	17						-18	-7
14		29				-22		-11
5	12				-52		-4	-15
7			57					11
13	22						-11	-3
9		28				-30		-8
10	6						-19	-14
-4								-5

PUZZLE#65
SOLUTION

12	8						9	5
-4		-14				27		4
-12	-22				11		18	7
-10			-25					11
3	-8			0			1	-1
-11		-11				-16		2
10	-3						-17	-2
-13								-15
1	-2		46		-32		-20	-14
-3		4				-44		-6
-9	6						-24	-8
15								-16
6	19						-12	-5
13		42				12		-7
14	23						24	8
9								16

PUZZLE#66
SOLUTION

4	-3						8	2
-7		-1				-4		6
-5	2				-14		-12	-1
7			-29					-11
-16	-22			0			-2	-12
-6		-28				-10		10
9	-6						-8	5
-15								-13
8	22		20		23		18	3
14		5				32		15
-14	-17						14	16
-3								-2
13	3						4	-8
-10		15				-9		12
11	12						-13	-4
1								-9

Challenging Thirty-two Solutions

PUZZLE#67
SOLUTION

5	12						1	-3
7		22				-22		4
-1	10						-23	-14
11			45		-34			-9
6	-4					-9		-11
-10		23				-12		2
13	27						-3	10
14				0				-13
3	-5						31	15
-8		-6				36		16
1	-1						5	-7
-2			-20		9			12
-5	4						-8	8
9		-14				-27		-16
-12	-18						-19	-4
-6								-15

PUZZLE#68
SOLUTION

13	2						1	-9
-11		29				-22		10
11	27				-33		-23	-8
16			47					-15
-4	11						-3	7
15		18				-11		-10
12	7						-8	-13
-5				0				5
2	3						6	-2
1		-6				16		8
3	-9						10	6
-12			-26		12			4
-7	-13						-17	-14
-6		-20				-4		-3
9	-7						13	14
-16								-1

PUZZLE#69
SOLUTION

9	25					6		4
16		21			1			2
7	-4					-5		10
-11			37	-19				-15
-4	2				-13			-3
6		16		-20				-10
15	14				-7			-2
-1			0					-5
-8	5					-2		14
13		18		-23				-16
1	13				-21			-14
12			15	-33				-7
8	19					-18		-6
11		-3		-10				-12
-9	-22				8			3
-13								5

PUZZLE#70
SOLUTION

4	-7					21		12
-11		-8		16				9
1	-1				-5			-15
-2			7	-26				10
3	10				-25			-13
7		15		-42				-12
-9	5				-17			-1
14			0					-16
11	6					4		8
-5		-9		13				-4
-8	-15				9			-6
-7			-11	30				15
-3	2				-12			-14
5		-2		17				2
-10	-4				29			13
6								16

Challenging Thirty-two Solutions

PUZZLE#71
SOLUTION

-14	-19						-15	-6
-5		-6				-29		-9
6	13						-14	-13
7			29		-45			-1
13	28						-24	-16
15		35				-16		-8
-4	7						8	5
11				0				3
1	-2						5	12
-3		-25				4		-7
-11	-23						-1	9
-12			-8		24			-10
8	22						2	4
14		17				20		-2
-15	-5						18	16
10								2

PUZZLE#72
SOLUTION

7	2						28	12
-5		-19				36		16
-14	-21						8	-6
-7			-7		40			14
-12	-2						-5	-11
10		12				4		6
13	14						9	11
1				0				-2
3	-12						-4	4
-15		-6				19		-8
9	6						23	8
-3			-24		-9			15
2	7						-17	-4
5		-18				-28		-13
-16	-25						-11	-1
-9								-10

BQ Sixty-four Puzzle Solutions

PUZZLE #73
SOLUTION

Leaves (L)	L2	L3	L4	L5	Root	R5	R4	R3	R2	Leaves (R)
-26	-15								22	24
11		-59						16		-2
-23	-44								-6	4
-21			-57				52			-10
16	-1								38	31
-17		2						36		7
-24	3								-2	-22
27			-64	28						20
-28	-20								47	30
8		-53						60		17
-8	-33								13	-1
-25			-7			-24				14
26	14								-39	-20
-12		46						-84		-19
10	32								-45	-15
22				0						-30
-32	-29								53	25
3		-48						40		28
-16	-19								-13	-4
-3			-104			84				-9
-31	-60								11	18
-29		-56						44		-7
-5	4								33	12
9			24	12						21
32	45								-31	-13
13		51						-14		-18
5	6								17	15
1			128			-72				2
23	29								-41	-27
6		77						-58		-14
19	48								-17	-6
29										-11

Easy Sixty-four Solutions

PUZZLE #74
SOLUTION

-5									43	12
29	24							81		31
3		47							38	24
20	23		98				107			14
22									55	32
18	40	51					26			23
15									-29	-16
-4	11		4	160						-13
-27									6	-3
-23	-50	-37					-5			9
2									-11	-18
11	13		-94				53			7
-24									42	16
8	-16	-57					58			26
-11				0					16	28
-30	-41									-12
-10									28	30
-20	-30	-52					14			-2
-7									-14	-8
-15	-22		-47				1			-6
13									31	4
-1	12	5					-13			27
-17									-44	-19
10	-7		-101	-63						-25
-9									27	6
17	8	-53					-18			21
-29									-45	-31
-32	-61		-54				-64			-14
19									3	-22
1	20	-1					-46			25
-26									-49	-28
5	-21									-21

Page 81

Par Sixty-four Solutions

PUZZLE #75
SOLUTION

Col 1	Col 2	Col 3	Col 4	Col 5	Col 6	Col 7	Col 8	Col 9	Col 10	Col 11
-28	-46								50	27
-18		-7						87		23
32	39								37	9
7			46				95			28
30	52								10	-6
22		53						8		16
-9	1								-2	-21
10			97			58				19
-3	-14								-1	-25
-11		27						-4		24
20	41								-3	-4
21			51				-37			1
31	18								-40	-14
-13		24						-33		-26
18	6								7	5
-12				0						2
-16	-45								22	-7
-29		-103						14		29
-31	-58								-8	14
-27			-133				-22			-22
6	9								2	-2
3		-30						-36		4
-19	-39								-38	-8
-20			-66			-89				-30
26	16								-17	-32
-10		54						-23		15
13	38								-6	11
25			67				-67			-17
17	25								-20	-15
8		13						-44		-5
-24	-12								-24	-1
12										-23

PUZZLE #76

SOLUTION

Left	C2	C3	C4	C5	Center		RC4	RC3	RC2	Right
28	18	14	35	-7	0	12	49	20	5	29
-10										-24
-29	-4								15	11
25										4
16	-10	21						29	6	-15
-26										21
5	31								23	-9
26										32
18	2	-46	-42				-37	-3	-6	-25
-16										19
-21	-48								3	-7
-27										10
1	9	4						-34	-21	-8
8										-13
-14	-5								-13	-20
9										7
31	48	90	22	117		-122	-67	-32	8	-4
17										12
20	42								-40	-17
22										-23
-6	-18	-68						-35	17	3
-12										14
-32	-50								-52	-22
-18										-30
-11	19	32	95				-55	-39	-8	-31
30										23
-2	13								-31	-28
15										-3
13	37	63						-16	-17	2
24										-19
-1	26								1	-5
27										6

Ultimate Challenge Solution

PUZZLE#77
SOLUTION

7										23
-25	-18								37	14
11		-33						56		-11
-26	-15								19	30
-7			-111				106			20
-18	-25								42	22
-29		-78						50		-5
-24	-53								8	13
25				-152		18				-22
-2	23								-49	-27
-1		28						-84		-20
6	5								-35	-15
-19			-41				-88			-23
-31	-50								-11	12
9		-69						-4		-21
-28	-19								7	28
5					0					32
29	34								15	-17
26		91						40		1
31	57								25	24
3			101				35			-14
-4	-1								4	18
-10		10						-5		4
21	11								-9	-13
-6				45		89				-3
15	9								14	17
-12		-12						6		8
-9	-21								-8	-16
2			-56				54			19
-32	-30								46	27
16		-44						48		10
-30	-14								2	-8

Page 84

About the Author

Whit McMahan is an IT Specialist, programmer, and part-time actor living in Nashville, TN. Whit holds a B.S. Degree in Computer Science and holds several computer networking certifications. By experimenting with recursive addition on certain sets of integers, he developed the concept for the Balance Quest puzzle.

Besides puzzles, Whit enjoys traveling, participating in "Civil War" reenactments, and the great out-of-doors.